WHO'S AT HOME?
Maggie Silver

MATHEW PRICE LIMITED

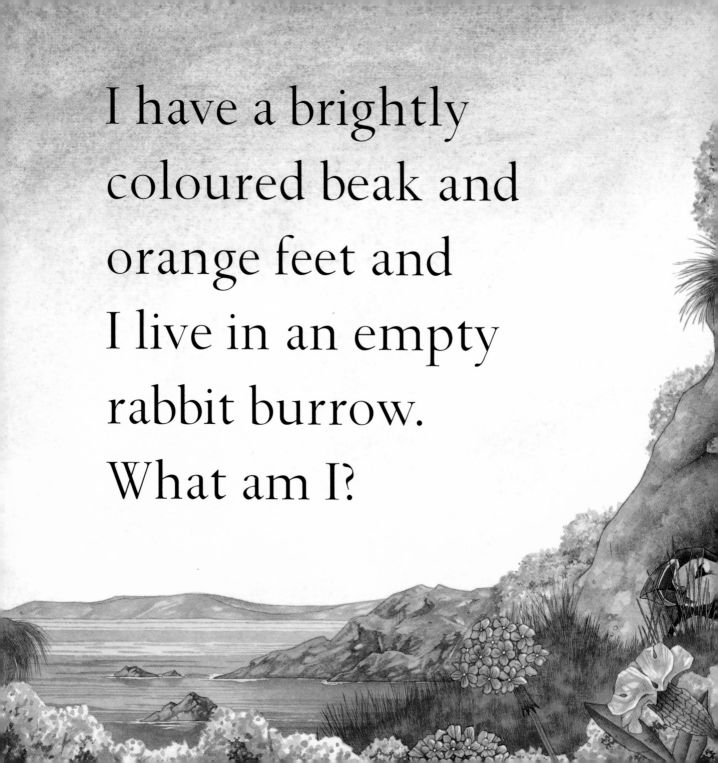

I have a brightly
coloured beak and
orange feet and
I live in an empty
rabbit burrow.
What am I?

I'm very small but I have big eyes to help me see at night. I live inside a prickly cactus.
What am I?

We are not birds but we can fly. We like to sleep beneath a leaf high in the trees.

What are we?

We love to play in the river. We can swim very fast. Our home is in the river bank. What are we?

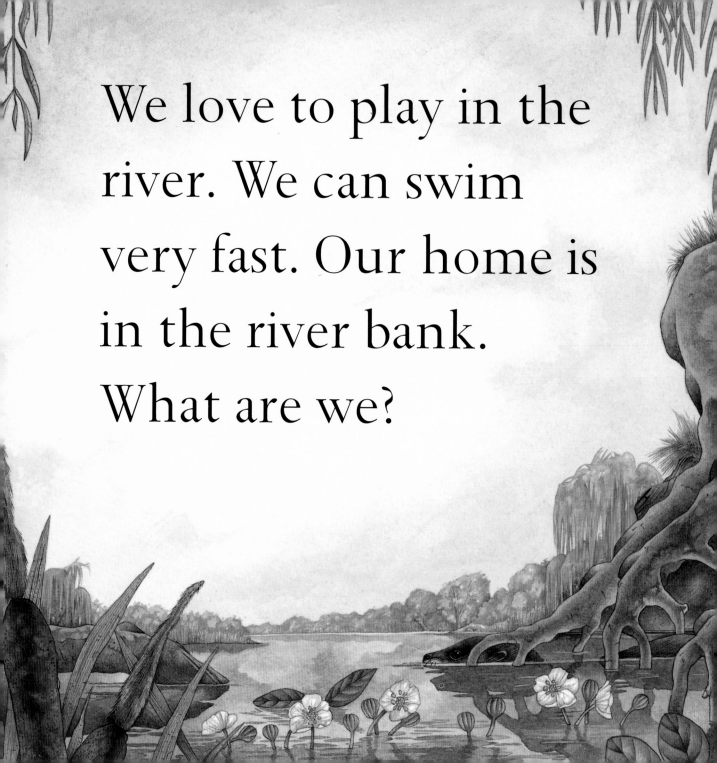

I have no legs but I can move quickly. I'm red and yellow and black and I live under a rock. What am I?

I have four legs and a
long bushy tail. I
live high up inside
a hollow tree.
What am I?

I swim in the ocean but I am not a fish. I have eight arms and I live in an old jug.
What am I?

I'm very strong and very fierce. I live with my family in a cave in the jungle.
What am I?

FACT FILES

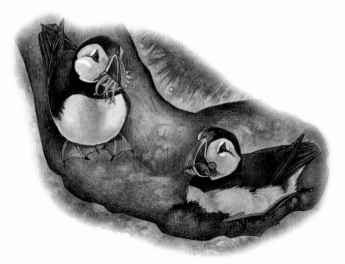

A cliff top in Scotland

Puffins are birds but they can swim as well as they can fly. They nest in burrows on the cold shores of the North Atlantic and usually lay one egg. They eat fish.

A desert in South West America

This tiny owl has found a very safe home in a prickly cactus. It hunts at night and lives of insects and other small creatures, such as mice. It is five and a half inches (fourteen centimetres) long.

A jungle in South America

Tent bats chew across the spine of a leaf until it folds down over them like a tent. They shelter there during the day and at night go out and eat fruit.

A river bank in Europe

Otters love to play in and out of the river. They make mudslides and splash down into the water. They have webbed feet, so they swim very fast under water. They eat fish and shellfish.

An American woodland

Scarlet kingsnakes are harmless. They are very shy and hardly ever come out during the day. They hide under stones and bits of bark and come out at night to hunt small animals like mice and lizards. They lay anything from 2 to 6 eggs.

A South American jungle

This is a Golden Lion Tamarin, a small monkey that lives in the forests of Brazil. In the daytime it eats fruit and insects. At night it likes to find a hollow tree to sleep in.